a chronology of blood

Mary Burritt Christiansen Poetry Series

Mary Burritt Christiansen Poetry Series
HILDA RAZ, SERIES EDITOR

The Mary Burritt Christiansen Poetry Series publishes two to four books a year that engage and give voice to the realities of living, working, and experiencing the West and the Border as places and as metaphors. The purpose of the series is to expand access to, and the audience for, quality poetry, both single volumes and anthologies, that can be used for general reading as well as in classrooms.

Also available in the Mary Burritt Christiansen Poetry Series:

small lives: poems by Gary Jackson
A Real Man Would Have a Gun: Poems by Stacey Waite
Dream of the Bird Tattoo: Poems and Sueñitos by Juan J. Morales
Unruly Tree: Poems by Leslie Ullman
A Walk with Frank O'Hara: Poems by Susan Aizenberg
Light of Wings: Poems by Sarah Kotchian
Trials and Tribulations of Dirty Shame, Oklahoma: And Other Prose Poems by Sy Hoahwah
A Guide to Tongue Tie Surgery: Poems by Tina Carlson
Point of Entry: Poems by Katherine DiBella Seluja
Victory Garden: Poems by Glenna Horton Luschei

For additional titles in the Mary Burritt Christiansen Poetry Series, please visit unmpress.com.

a chronology of blood

poems

TEO SHANNON

UNIVERSITY OF NEW MEXICO PRESS | ALBUQUERQUE

Printed in the United States of America

ISBN 978-0-8263-6868-3 (paper)
ISBN 978-0-8263-6869-0 (ePub)

Library of Congress Control Number: 2025932512

Founded in 1889, the University of New Mexico sits on the traditional homelands of the Pueblo of Sandia. The original peoples of New Mexico—Pueblo, Navajo, and Apache—since time immemorial have deep connections to the land and have made significant contributions to the broader community statewide. We honor the land itself and those who remain stewards of this land throughout the generations and also acknowledge our committed relationship to Indigenous peoples. We gratefully recognize our history.

Cover illustration: *The Sacrifice of Isaac*, 1602, by Caravaggio
Designed by Felicia Cedillos
Composed in Sabon LT Std

for survivors, especially the angry ones

If I cannot air this pain and alter it, I will surely die of it.

—AUDRE LORDE

Contents

i

Lengua

I've forgotten how to speak

so I eat lengua. I wrap it in a tortilla.

The cow speaks for me,

says:
    You ate my cheapest part,
says:
    Wouldn't you rather taste my loin?
says:
    I was raised on corn and secret beatings,
says:
    I did not eat by choice,
says:
    They cut out my tongue only after they cut my throat,
says:
    It is good you do not speak,
says:
    I will speak with my grief-tongue for you.

Arrival

What I want to tell you is that Sarah made me a toy from the beginning. I was a burp-your-baby doll. When you tilted me, my eyes rolled back. I was a plaything. When Mom came home from the hospital under a Scorpio sun, Sarah wanted to hold me. What I want you to know is how she turned to Mom and told her she hated her. I want you to know it began there. I don't have a beginning or a creation: I have an arrival in Sarah's arms.

Sarah, Age 11

I am hunting you.
Daddy brought home Bambi.
I told him not to get blood on that meat.
Mother has to cook it for dinner. Red meat,
I am hunting you.

You dumb little boy,
thinking you can run or hide.
I love to squish you
in between the washer and dryer.
No Daddy or Mother when the sun's out,
you dumb little boy.

Just listen to me:
Take off your pants.
I want to see your blood and your meat.
Kiss inside my pants. Kiss this hair. Kiss this.
It's okay, shut up,
just listen to me:

Tonight, extra dessert.
Don't I taste sweet too?
I love you, maybe, underneath me.
Daddy's in the garage. He smells like smoke.
Tonight, I'll make dinner,
and I'll give you extra dessert.

Fear

In Florida, I loved magnolias—
their blossoms like felt blades, large and fragrant.

When closed, they were pretend grenades,
weapons of the playground, ammo for devils.

My brown skin was pretend, too.
Pretend enemy, pretend dead.

And Sarah, somehow, was an ally. Mulch turned to bullets
and fists to bombs as we fought

for our lordship over the slides and swings.
We waged many wars against those children,

unwilling allies, necessary comrades. Traitors, too.
I feared those kids like I fear Sarah now,

like I will always fear the white-hot moment
a beautiful thing transforms into pain.

Sarah as Grendel

I can hear the carpet outside shift.
Please, stomach, don't echo her growls.
I wasn't fast enough to get the phone this time.
I am alone in this mead hall: sink, toilet, tub,
spinning wildly in the oarlock of panic.
Mist is coming under the door. Breath
of bananas and blood. If I curl up in the tub,
my sweat will join the cold puddle of the morning.
If I turn off the light, maybe I can measure
her shadow steps, count each softening claw
as she stalks away, escape to my room,
try to snatch a lifeline. Anything
to avoid her teeth. Anything at all.

Knife Spell

I'll tell you what happened backward
to erase the memory:
Boy,
you've got the knife.
Daddy comes in. I practice tears.
You are shaking. You are screaming.
Your eyes shock-white.
You pull the knife out of the block.
Chili dogs boiling.
I chase you to the kitchen.
Daddy's in the garage.
I've got you in the living room.
Mother won't be back for dinner.
You're alone.
I come out of my room.

I'm hungry.

Doll Play

Magic color-changing body, she dips you into water,
watches you change from brown to red. The water

turns red too. Little plastic heart. Little plastic boy
with snap-on clothes and eyes that really follow you.

Parts small enough to choke on. Parts not intended
for internal use. Articulated limbs, they really bend!

Little girls like Sarah play with little dolls. Little dolls
are alive at night, and they cry at how they got bent.

Why do you think they trap them in plastic cases?
Or hide them between the furniture, the laundry machines?

We play at house, at love. Little brothers
and little plastic boys. Why make-believe when

you have life's realest doll right here in your hands?

.30-06 (Thirty Aught Six)

In high school, I shot my father's guns. The recoil
sent the butt of one into my nose, cutting it open.
At school, a teacher praised me for being a man.

By then, I was sick with guns. Since childhood,
we were forced an hour south to Ocala to shoot
into the bare hillside and at paper targets while white men
with gray beards, Oakley shades, and boxes of ammo
dipped their hands into coolers of Bud Light.

At the range, one man would call it hot, then cold,
would urge us out to the field to check how close we got
to shooting the chest of a black silhouette,
something Sarah was in love with: the power, the threat,
the unmistakable sulfur of the spent shells littering the sand.

Later, my father told me her obsession frightened him.
When he laid out his thirty-something guns,
Sarah picked up the assault rifle, heavy stock on her shoulder,
put her eye to the scope, and aimed.

Sarah as Dracula

I've lost a lot of blood in my time.
By doctors, by men, by her. In the dark
she rests on the earth of her homeland:
stained blankets, reeking mattresses.
When she fled her castle, I followed
to stake her heart, to cut her neck.
We found troves of her beloveds:
lewd displays of women and men
packed in trunks and tubs, a library
of lust. I found the trophies of my body there.
I found the trap of fangs, the designs
of a monster. I begged to God,
wreathed myself in His sacraments,
hoped it would ward her from my door.

High Quality Tattoo 8 × 6″ Blank Practice Skin for Beginners and Experienced Artists

flexible and has a similar feel as human skin

I tell some friends about practice skins,
about a friend that apprenticed for a while
and showed her progress on Instagram.
Tattooing is a trade and an art like anything else,
but you fail to see the work of practice.
You fail to understand that the medium
demands a body for the experiment.
How to practice a permanent art?
You need willing skin or a substitute.
Even reckless, rebellious teenagers try
their stick-and-pokes on citrus peels. So
someone clever invented these skins,
which feel no pain as you drive the needles in,
marking them forever. You see where I'm going with this, right?
The skin which has been practiced on,
and the skin which has not.

Boy Found Dead

for all the dead boys

2-year-old boy found dead in Wayne, Mich., home, parents' location unknown

standing at the edge of stairs gives me vertigo now

Missing Spanish boy found dead in car

but when I crawl to the drop-off, I want to jump

Teenage boy among 4 found dead in apparent murder-suicide

I want to see the blood angel my limp frame would make.

Boy found dead in trash was killed by "unspecified" means

who would find me? what animal would find me first?

Agency finds records altered after boy found dead

what would be said of me? how long

No foul play suspected after missing boy found dead

would the stain last on the cement?

Boy, 2, found dead in Choctaw County pond

then I dream of drowning. I dream

Charges pending for father after boy, 2, found dead in Little Village

of slipping into the darkness of an alleyway

Baby boy found dead in playground trash can in Queens

always hunted, then disposed of.

Boy, 2, found dead in pool

most of all I dream of Sarah

17-year-old boy found dead was shot

wonder if I was the only one she hunted

Boy found dead in San Antonio motel

I don't know about her life anymore. I know sometimes

Boy, 2, found dead in Chicago home with throat cut

when the deer escapes, the hunter moves on

Man arrested after woman and 15-year-old boy found slain

but sometimes, the hunter follows for days.

Missing boy of homeless Marysville woman found dead in Mexico

this is called pursuit predation. the fear takes over

Playing truant, boy found dead near school

and the prey gives out, paralyzed by the never-safety.

Missing Juárez boy found dead in field

then the hunter dances around her fire.

Sarah as Mr. Hyde

She was kind. She was unkind.
She fed me. She starved me.
She protected me. She beat me.
She possessed me. She abandoned me.
She obsessed over me. She ignored me.
She nursed me. She cursed me.
She clothed me. She stripped me.
She followed me. She follows me.

Self-Portrait as Fears Manifested in Dreams

When Mom dies, I can't let Sarah touch anything. I know she'll want everything she can take. Mom tells me there's a list on the back of her will. My father is irrelevant. I know he'll die long before Mom does. All I have to do is survive them both. Have I ever told you about the dreams I have? The scene changes, but I'm always carrying something heavy or my body gets heavier. The closer I am to waking up, the heavier it gets. I stumble. I fall. I'm often chased. I have this dream at least twice a week. I think it's my sleep paralysis, which I thought I'd drugged away. I'm afraid I'm used to the drugs. In Baltimore, I dreamt I took a flight to Germany when my friend was there because I missed her and I was drinking three bottles of wine a day. I had to call Mom to check my bank account, to see if I'd bought a ticket and left. I have dreams about money. About lack of money. Mom told me we were poor when I was in grade school, and it stuck. She's an accountant like that. I thought I had to shoulder everything. I still do. I have dreams about trying shrooms because I've scared myself off all the worse things, or I've done those worse things. Every time I make a morning ritual, I change it in case my dreams copy it. I'm afraid one day I won't know what's real. Often I don't sleep. Then I sleep away whole weeks. The dishes pile up, the litter box goes un-scooped. I feel good about myself when I take the recycling down four flights to the dumpster, as if it's a feat, as if normal people struggle with basic chores. When I can't sleep, I imagine a world in which I have superpowers: mind reading, telekinesis—like a need to know the truth, a need to be stronger than I am. Then I fall asleep, and my haunts come back. I lose my powers, the villain kills me, I watch endless people die. What is the measure of a good person if by nature I am a miserable person? I try to do good, to be good, but I have dreams where I'm the murderer. I wrote a poem about slamming wine bottles onto the concrete floor of a store, and it went into my dream. I wrote poems with knives, and so many dreams have knives. I hold back shouting at my father or my sister, so I only shout in my dreams. Whole dreams where I do nothing but scream. Sometimes Mom is dead in these dreams. Or worse, she takes their side. In my dreams, Sarah is always there. In my dreams, Sarah's hands chase me. In my dreams, Sarah's mouth is moving, and all I can focus on is the spit webbing across her lips. Sometimes I wake up, and Sarah is there.

Sheep's Brain

In biology, we dissected a sheep's brain
preserved in formaldehyde. The stench
of the chemical made me gag
while, scalpel in hand, I sliced through
the cerebral fissure, divided
the brain in two hemispheres,
so we could identify the lobes, glands, places
of scientific inquiry. I remember plucking out
the pea-sized pituitary, my teacher telling me my cuts
were clean, that I owed my skill to practice
in the kitchen, as if the cuts I made were
for a meal, as if we were doing more
than playing a game of make-believe scientists.
I suppose that's why I was handed the scalpel—
I was the one who curled my fingers
over the lobe like an onion and made the long,
terrible lines through the bleach-white organ.
Despite the smell, I was one of the few
that could handle the task, not make a joke of it.
The other boys stabbed at the gel-firm tissue,
punched ragged holes with the dull side of the blade.
The girls turned away, squealing, acting out their roles perfectly.
I was humorless, as humorless as I was
when I peeled the membranes from veal pancreases,
soaked them overnight in milk,
fried them for dinner. It was all necessary work to me,
to make good the meat of the dead.

I suppose my teacher was right: I had many hours
over a cutting board, knife in hand, to thank
for such beautiful halves of a sheep's brain,
two elegant pieces torn apart by curiosity.

Don't Remember

I'm missing days at a time. I'm missing weeks
in grade. I'm missing whatever happened
while Mom was in . I don't remember the .
I can't bring up the memories. I'm lost. I'm black oil
floating above water. I'm barely holding on.
I'm scared of what else I've made myself , what else
S might have done to me that no one will be able to
,
what other horrors this might be hiding from me, waiting
until it has to betray me.

Gallbladder

Sarah had her appendix out in August. Then
her gallbladder out on my birthday. Then
I was moved to a different school—
my seventh by this time.
When we rushed to the hospital
to remove the three-centimeter stone
and her useless organ, I felt nothing.
I complained about my ruined birthday
out of obligation. There was nothing special
about turning fourteen. Sarah had finished
having her fun with me a year or two before.
I wasn't worried about Sarah's surgery.
I wasn't wishing she'd suffer. I was waiting
for the next thing, whatever it might be.
High school, college, a knight in shining armor.
The next thing would come eventually.
Then something else after that.

Her Bedroom

She squirrelled away Tupperware,
stashed food between the bookshelf and the wall.
Hid GladWare in the closet under sweaters and laundry.
Our dog bit through her door, chewed the corner-wood free.
There was a maggoty sandwich sandwiched behind the dresser.
We tore it down: tore down the wall, the bed,
ripped the mattress, lit up the dark closet.
Clothes, papers, toys and wrappers and bags.
All manner of debris. Putrid, oozing blankets,
pillows of crust, dull crowns of dust.
Puzzle-piece portrait of dolls, frozen in frame,
their porcelain counterparts lining the walls.
Doll after doll, blank glass eyes. One, a nun,
patron of this disaster. Dog hair, sticky notes,
Lip Smacker ChapSticks, a broken ballerina music box.
The snapped blinds, the window screen ripped out.
A computer riddled with viruses from downloading porn.
An erotic novel she was writing saved on the desktop,
Harlequin romances hid under the bed.
A whale poster in the closet, the sweater Mom knit
with angora hot air balloons. Oh, and the smell.
I can't forget the smell. The worst of it all
was the sweet-sick of her body spray
trying to cover up the rot. Vanilla. Brown sugar.
I'm ruined for sweet candles and perfumed friends.
When I open leftovers in the fridge, I gag. When I smell
bananas, I have to leave the room. Me, gloved, trash bag in hand,
packing away the rotten moraine left behind her.
All of this a portrait of her, her heart, my skin on display.

Sarah as Dr. Frankenstein

She stitches me together: her own
sexually functioning marvel. She shoots me
full of lightning. She props me up
and teaches me letters until
I outgrow her mind. I teach myself
math and God and words.
She takes pistols and daggers to hunt me,
so I flee to ice and shipwreck.
I cut apart her loved ones. I cut
all mortal ties. In the end,
I let the fog take me.

Kindness

Tired, sore, shoulders broken
by luggage, feet broken
by city sidewalks, the train,
the car, the walk up to my parents'
home—at last I can rest.

At last, the sofa is mine,
the night descended already
like the cover of a birdcage,
ready to signal pause, comfort,
the ceasing of the day's fraught travel.

At last I can lie down across the cushions,
and my father comes in with a blanket.
Handing it to me, soft, warm fleece, a comfort
every home that might be a home should offer.
He says to me, *I washed it*
because your sister used it last.

The surprise of the kindness, the gesture,
small as it may be. The gathering
of the laundry, the cleaning of soiled things,
the chore he leaves in arrogance for Mom.
Look how he cares, in this moment, how he cares
enough to strip the fabric of its past,
to make it new again for my body,
which is not a new body
and hasn't been for so long

that it can't remember
the sensation of newness.

He leaves with a *goodnight*
I receive as the largest gift
he's ever given, from the man whose hand
held fists, whose arms held affection at length,
whose back held the tight knots of anger.
He's gone up the creaking stairs
and left me here, holding a blanket,
freshly cleaned. How warm, how soft,
how easily I sleep that night.

You Call Your Mother and Hear Terrible News

and you are made a child again. Your mother
is withholding information for your well-being.

She hasn't called you in two days while your father
is confronting his darkest fears.

Everyone is failing to be a good person.
Everyone feels responsible for something they didn't do.

Now it all makes sense: Sarah who raped you
might have been raped by Uncle Don.

Now Uncle Don is running from the police to your parents,
expecting sanctuary, except your parents already know the story.

Your father exchanges money for the three guns in Uncle Don's truck,
enough for hotel, gas, and food, and tries to send him back to Seattle

to face the consequences of touching a little girl.
Uncle Don touched a little girl and her name was Sarah.

Sarah touched you, and it all makes sense.
You know Sarah wasn't ever right,

but you didn't know what made her not right.

Now your father worries Don has another gun.
Uncle Don says he might have another one hidden.

You wait a few months and Google Uncle Don,
and the first result is Inmate Detail: One Count

Child Molestation, Booking Date April 2019, Total Bond
Set at $100,000.00 for Flight Risk. Felony Class B.

You Google what all of this means.
You Google the detention center.

You Google the county superior court proceedings
and find the arraignment and the affidavits, and you can buy them

for only $3.75, and you do. Your hands are shaking.
You are reading these documents in a coffee shop,

and you haven't told your mother you're reading them.
You're scared of what she might say, but you're more scared

of everything in the documents. You don't know the girlfriend
or the girlfriend's daughter. You read the email he sent before he
turned himself in:

He says he's sorry. He says he's praying to God. He says to put the phones
and TVs in her name. He says he's getting help. He says he loves her and her little girl too.

ii

First Sex

was a threesome on the Fourth of July. Yes; fireworks.
It was with a couple I trusted. I asked if they would help me.
Julio's arms were thick. Kyle's were thin.
Julio taught me to relax every muscle. Kyle
taught me how to kiss. Both taught me
how to clean up the mess. Did we use condoms?
I can't remember, but I know we showered together.
They told me they wanted to fuck me since freshman year.
I was seventeen and lonely. Julio smelled like the milk
he stocked at the grocery store. Kyle
was a student at the community college. They fucked me
many times after that night. Sometimes, Kyle would just watch.
I preferred that. I preferred the fantasy of a lover,
that Julio, with his thick arms, might be mine alone.
I shed my Catholic school uniform on their floor.
I took off my glasses.
How much was pity, giving into my pleas for grace?
I don't know what it means to do this. Or how to do this.
They never asked me to come over. I always did.

Sex After Conversion Therapy

When it was over, I could feel everything inside me
rise up, burn: acidic bile from an empty stomach
flooding a dry throat. I was sweaty, shaking,
the orgasm barely over, clawing at the toilet. Please,
let this be the last time. It's hard to breathe
with puke filling your mouth. I choked a lot
trying to find the bathroom in time.
I learned to start looking for it when I walked in.
There were men who thought I was disgusting,
who scowled at me from their doorways.
Others were concerned. One beautiful man,
whose tattoos told me he loved trees
and birds and silly quotes, held my waist.
He wet a washcloth and put it around my neck
and sat with me while I cried. How much
must come out of me tonight?
                                        Even years later,
as a lover kneels before me in a fluorescent-lit stall
of an anonymous bathroom, the fishhook of shame
pulls my stomach into my mouth. How long?
How many years has it been? Beneath me,
my man mistakes these wracking tremors for pleasure.

Daddy Porn

I want to know what makes me want to see
one man call another his "boy" and fuck him.
Oh, Freud would love this disaster.
I know I'm not the only one. It's a whole
godforsaken genre. How many times
has a hookup called me boy,
asked that I call him sir or Daddy? And look,
it worked. It got me into a jockstrap and out of the house
on a Wednesday night. God strike me down,
it was hot. I snuck out of my bedroom window
one college summer for fifteen musky minutes in his car,
and when I got back I hated myself for it.
In Chicago, there's a bar called Jackhammer
where downstairs you can't wear clothes.
You can only get drinks in plastic, so there's no glass.
Condoms are provided. There's a tub for piss—
a baptistry. This night—a sabbath for dangerous sex.
I once saw a man in ecstasy, sober, slung up
in a leather saddle and chains. His ass was bleeding,
but I couldn't look away. I walked closer to him,
saw his leg tattooed with the biohazard symbol.
His nipples were pierced. He screamed in pain,
but he kept saying, *Please, Daddy, more.*

Jeff and Kramer

At the corner of Clark and Touhy,
apartment N, N as in Nike,
there's a dog named Kramer.

Kramer watches *Indiana Jones*
and *Seinfeld* with his master.
White dog. White master.

Watches you fooled
into buying menthols, Gatorade,
withdrawing a hundred dollars in cash—
cash for GHB, Tina, maybe something else.

In a barricaded room,
Kramer whines, echoes,
No condoms. I'm a libertarian.

Kramer jumps over
the stacked boxes and cases,
sees your ass squeezed into
a neoprene singlet.

He mixes something for you,
lights a slim, clear pipe,
pins navy sheets against the sun-beat windows.

Put Kramer away.
Put Kramer away.
Come back and let me fuck you.

Thirty-six hours and no walk for Kramer.

Above Me, Jeff

presses my head to his crotch as if
he were petting Kramer. This touch
isn't demeaning. He is gentle with my head,
accepts what I think is the shape of affection
I am offering him.

I've asked him to show me
what form love takes in his world,
and while it contains a concentration of pain,
leaves me wracked, wrecked,
I can't fault him for his honesty.

Later, while he is inside me,
I tell him I love him. He asks me
what I said. Embarrassed, I repeat myself,
and he smiles as he puts his hands around my neck.

Jeff Forces Me to Have Sex with Strangers, Then Calls Me a Cheating Slut

and I wonder if I did cheat. If this
was all a test, that I was supposed to refuse

the man he presented to me. Like all dancers,
I worship my choreographer. I revere

the director of this pornography.
Jeff didn't want to call me his boyfriend,

told me how everyone he ever dated cheated.
The truth is, I cheated on R in high school.

I'm not innocent in all of this. Or maybe
I am innocent in this one place, here, in Chicago.

At this point, I've lost my sense of direction,
my excuse for falling into Jeff and staying there.

It seems so simple when he calls and tells me
I should go kill myself,

when I'm used to doing what he tells me to.

Man to Man

after Ai

I invite you to the bed, which
we will share for a short time. I've
bent the page of these sheets
in invitation, bookmarked it
for your body. Outside, the wind
of a flat prairie moves through this city,
one which was built tall in arrogance.
The wind rattles the brick and glass
like I will rattle you. Tonight,
I will have no mercy. No patience.
You walk toward me, rest the edge
of the sheet around your shoulders
like a mantle—a penitent with his veil
entering my confessional. I nod,
acknowledge the sins you'll commit in me.

Jackhammer

I've felt powerless for so long,
  glancing from one man's chest to his chin,
        never to his eyes,

to the next man, begging
  to be desired. I've worn the clothes
        they tell you not to wear outside

so long as someone looks at me.
  I go where the powerless go:
        downstairs, through the dark,

where your clothes are packed into brown bags,
  where an old man writes the bag number
        on your shoulder, so drunk

as you might become, you can't forget.
  Chicago is cold in the winter
        when all you're wearing

is a jockstrap and sneakers,
  cash for the bar tucked under a hat
        or a heel. Here,

I'm not powerless for the first time.
  Here, despite the men
        who won't look at me upstairs,

I'm shiny, new, already unwrapped
for their delight,
and for once

I decide who can look and who
can touch, and I want them all
to look and touch.

A man who looks like he could crush me
gently pulls at my waist,
and when I push his hand,

he walks away hungry.
I've never been a commodity,
desired like this, never

been able to deny the pleasure
of calloused fingertips.
Power is inverted here.

The men above, with their leather
and chains and latex,
are all performance.

Down here, even the tallest man
will kneel if I push on his shoulder,
if I grant him the gift

of service. Some men are proud. Proud
   until their knees touch unclean concrete.
         Others know to leave their pride upstairs.

Years Later, a Stranger Walks in Wearing the Same Cologne as Jeff

In Southeast Asia
the carnivorous pitcher-plant
mimics the scent of flowers
in its leaves, dissolves
its prey, and leaves
no trace

On My Birthday I Witness a Car Accident

I'm on the corner of the sidewalk and it's raining,
because of course it must be. For the car
to run the red light, for the darkness of 7:00 p.m.,
for the crunch-splash-shatter of the impact,
for the metaphor, it must be. I am on the corner
of the sidewalk, waiting to cross so I can drink beer
and read a book alone, surrounded by strangers
with no interests or stakes in me. I do this often—
reading by myself among the drinking.

Is it gauche to compare the beer taps to rain? The trajectory
of my life to that SUV? The relatively good outcome—
no injuries, no one going too fast, just smashed front ends—
to how I survive despite my best attempts at self-destruction?
If it is, well, I've gone and done it, haven't I?
I've put the words down, as if I'm not desperate for you
to tell me it's okay, to forgive my lack of art here.

I have a confession: I called 911 and detailed the accident,
crossed the street and drank two beers. Then I took a cab
to a hotel where a man I've never met told me I was a good boy
and whispered *Happy Birthday* when he finished.

Touch-Starved

for Ryan

We both know what is light
is not light alone—no light
without heat and those attracted to it.
This is not a poem
about moths and flames
or ugly creatures fluttering
around their tragic ends.
The moth knows what happens—
bears witness to the others
dropping from the air like heavy feathers
full of dust. The moth isn't here
because of an attraction, but hunger,
unbearable lack of nectar, unbearable
thirst for the Pentecostal vision.
The moth burns his hands
holding the light. The wicked
inherit light with pain—
the wicked, with their capes of scales,
finally turning to a salvation
that cuts across their eyes.
Listen, the moth isn't turning
to light for fascination,
for untamable curiosity.
The moth is desperate
as I am desperate, burning:
How do I ask you to touch me?

My Therapist Tells Me I'm Resilient

My file number is 17149, and I know it better than she does.
She requests Consultation Room B, and she'll get it
because we meet in it every week. There's a white-noise machine
in the hall. Room B is the biggest. The observation mirror
is the smallest. But I know I'm not observed. I know
she's read my poems. Her professor-doctor has read my poems.
She tells me I'm resilient. I'm rational. I'm mature. I've calculated
the impact of every social interaction. I'm a good kid. I'm
stronger than most in the trauma clinic. I'm ready
to leave. She's given me a worksheet every session:
Do I dream? Am I dying? Do the dead wish to kill me?
Do I sleep? Do I go back in time? Do I fear men who can kill?
Am I easily startled? Am I anxious? Have I seen anyone die?
And I tally my scores, numbers to join others in my head.
File: 17149. Hours of sleep in the last week: 6. Score: 38.

I Accidentally Tell a Man I've Just Met "I Love You" While He Is Inside Me

and the first thing he says after he finishes is *Did you realize you said that?*
and of course I didn't, but I know it's a thing liable to happen.

Liable to happen—that I am full of tremendous feelings I hate,
and one of those is love. If I've had any amount of wine, you can tell

because I love you. Even in distress, I do so love. I've done this before.
I told Jeff the same thing, the day he broke up with me. Isn't it lovely,

having all of this to contain—all of my feelings? Last night,
the man, whose name I can't remember, did what must be done

to the kind of body I have, the kind of body that begs to be so sweetly punished.
In every case, I am lying belly up and vulnerable, heart closest to heart

which beats in his chest, down to himself, into me so that I must acknowledge it.
It's an exchange like anything else. I can make vows against the hammer

but love the tempering. The strength of the hammer, though,
is in the flattening, the dulling, the beating. The hammer makes anything

its own drum, the first of which was skin impossibly stretched across clay.
I am skin wrapped around bones—perhaps why when the hammer strikes,

even if accidentally, I beat: *I love you, I love you.*

Jeff, One Last Time

I know it won't be the last time
that I love this way.
I am a zoetrope/gif/
never-ending matryoshka
of beating myself into a corner.
After I let him convince me
that meth could be fun for sex;
after he thought I cheated on him
with a man he ordered me to fuck;
after he called me trash, told me
not to speak to him, only be a toy;
after we'd been broken up for a while;
after I unblocked his number;
after I got back in town;
after I hadn't touched anyone
since I last touched him;
after I said I wouldn't do it again;
even after everything,
I begged him again and again and again
for one last time.

Worship

You can kneel anywhere
and make a shrine of it,
as long as there is room to kneel.

I don't believe in god
but in other forms of worship,
which are nothing more than dedication:

the care with which you must hold a knife,
or the hours spent sharpening the blade,
every task a meditation in precision.

I have spent hours in the house of a man
who, like any benevolent god,
must mark his benevolence

by meting out punishment
on the wicked. And I am the wicked.
I have been the wicked for so long

it has become my only name.

Years Later, Someone Tells Me the Truth About Moths

That they aren't attracted to light. They
have no desire to self-immolate, to die
by flame or lightbulb or electric zapper.
It's a reflex—they can't help themselves—
reorienting to the artificial sun at their back.
But in doing so, they enter a cruel spiral around the light
to keep themselves on the right path. You see,
gravity means little to a moth so small, so light.
So the sun, moon, stars—and now your porch light—
guide them upright. I was wrong when I told you
the moth was desperate for touch. I was wrong
about its fascination. I was right about the pain.
I was right about the tragedy. I didn't know, then,
that every love, like a lamp, traps someone.

iii

You Call Your Mother and Hear Terrible News

Again. This time, it's worse. Your father is in jail.
This time the county records say

Domestic Assault Felony by Strangulation
with a mug shot of your father, head freshly shaved.

Your mother is safe now, but she tells you the whole story:
Your father went wild, lost his mind, cut his hand

taking the car keys off the hook, bled on your mother's neck
while he crushed her throat. She told him she was dying,

and he said *Maybe You Should.* The car alarm went off,
and she made a break for it, got to the bedroom to call 911

before he kicked the door in. You have pictures of the broken door
on your phone now. The police do too. And her throat. And the blood

like breadcrumbs, every place he's put his hands. Somehow,
you aren't surprised. And neither are your friends who knew him.

It took thirty-four years, but it was a matter of time. It is January 15,
2022, at sunrise.
The sun climbs higher in the sky.

Summer of ’96

Disneyland, California. The summer
Aunt Heidi fainted from the heat. The summer
I fell in love with Esmerelda. The summer,
with the rest of us away, my father drank himself
into a stupor, passed out on the floor. A summer
when Sarah was untouched and innocent. I remember
Disney autograph books, a train conductor’s cap,
the runaway Jet Ski, the Pirates of the Caribbean ride.
For Mom, it was three weeks without a demand for sex.
Three weeks away from four jobs
and being told it wasn’t enough. The first time
(with a three- and six-year-old on each hip)
she asked herself if she should leave him.

Not Everything Needs to Be a Poem

is what I like to tell myself when I notice
my father is missing in ██████ in my stories.
It's not a metaphor. He wasn't disappearing
for the cliché cigarettes or a gallon of milk from the corner store.
I can assure you, we all felt his presence. I mean
we all felt his fists at one time or ██████.
No one was allowed to play the piano when he got ████.
No one was allowed to bother him in the █████.
No one was allowed to have an opinion unless it was ███.
Simple laws any tyrant would enforce.
Not everything needs to be ██████. Not how I've tried my hand
at analogies for the way he punched me in the face,
going eighty miles an hour on the highway to breakfast,
when I told him he didn't understand me. I've tried to explain
the aftermath of that morning, tried to talk about my jaw
and how it still clicks. Not everything needs ██████████.
Not everything ██████████████. Not the time this year
when I got mad and pointed a fork while I was cooking
and he almost beat me again. Not
██████████████████████████.
Not a list of ██████ I can hardly remember, not all the times
he broke open my door, not all the times I dreamed of running away,
not every time I wish he'd ███, or they'd divorce, or whatever my heart
was set on that day. Not everything can be a poem.

And After All That, He Laughs at Such a Funny Joke

In a house on Erskine Street that I don't remember,
my mother makes bacon. Everyone has breakfast.
It's a normal Sunday. I am about a year old,
weaned, teething on pizza crusts, eating real food.
Mom says I might have been eating something like bacon
by then, but I don't know. I do know she made enough,
that everyone had their fill, that there were even
a few pieces leftover. So while my father showers
and Mom cleans up, she gives the leftover bacon
to me or Sarah or herself. It doesn't really matter, does it?
The bacon is gone now. When my father comes back out
and nothing is there, no one should be surprised.
Except he is. He's surprised that at the end of the meal,
the food would be put away, and for whatever reason,
that angers him. I don't have any memory of this,
but the way Mom tells it to me, I can see it:
red in the face, tight-set jaw, clenched fists, arms, shoulders,
white-wide eyes you might confuse for astonishment.
His eyes always went wide in fury. They didn't narrow
like the villains I read about in my books. And after the eyes,
the vibrating, like he caught a sudden chill, shivering
before he let loose his hands. I was there but I don't remember.
Uncle Don stops him before he can do too much,
but it's enough. It's Sunday.

On Monday, Mom goes out,
buys all the bacon she can afford. All twelve pounds of it.
Every penny she can spare before the next paycheck.
Stacks it up in the freezer so it falls out when he goes to get ice.

Boar Hanging in Florida, August

The skin cut open looks like
the underside of embroidery.

There's more blood in the body
than you'd think. Some always gets out.

When my father caught wild boars
in a Florida forest overrun with them,

he built a gallows for the bloodletting.
He had to keep watch all night—

raccoons eat more than just scraps.
With all the light he shone on the corpses,

it was as if a museum of natural history
had commissioned the display.

Once drained, they were skinned—
our black dog dancing with lust.

Good Friday Boat

My father wants a boat before we have a home.
Our first house came in two halves on the back of a truck.
We're moving now to a place with its own curses,
ones we didn't make: the termite-ridden siding,
the urine-stained carpets, the dusty-rose toilets.
We paint it new with the money of Mom's dead uncle.
We use every last penny.
We make ourselves poor again,
but we have real mattresses. My father
wants a garage with a fourteen-foot car lift, and he gets it.
My father wants a boat, one he'll barely use.
He thinks everything is unfair because
Mom won't give him thousands of dollars
we don't have. It's Good Friday, and we're on our way
to confession. On the side of the road: *Look,*
like a sign, Mom says, *a boat for sale.*

Trajectory

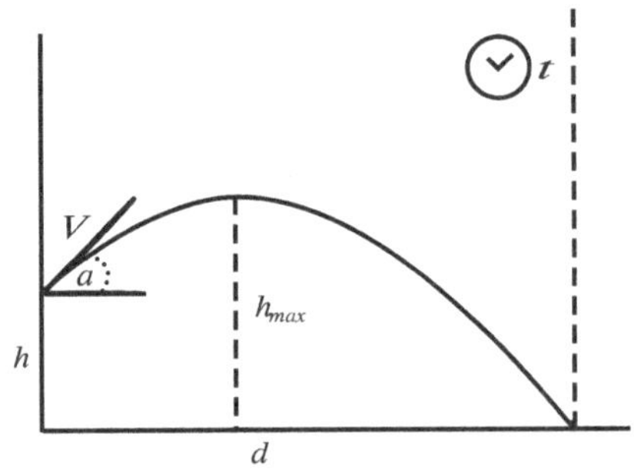

where *t*
is equal to Mother's Day, 2009,
when he finds the takeout is missing eggrolls

where *h*
is equal to my mother's height, 5′2″,
lifted several inches off the ground by her neck

where *V*
is to be solved, the velocity at which he threw her,
enough force to shake the house

where *d*
is equal to the distance from garage door to pantry,
not far, but far enough

where *hmax*
is equal to meeting my eyes midair,
less than the doorframe

where *a*
  is equal to the angle to land her through the doors,
  under the shelves, under cans and bags of flour,
  snacks, pasta, sugar, bags of dog food, the Tupperware
  she used to sell to make ends meet

Interview with a Glacier

I heard you were dying.
I am not dying. I am calving.

What does it mean to calve?
It means I shed. I give way.

For what?
The ice in me is blue
because I cannot breathe.
When my great sides give way,
fall into the sea, I taste air again.

That isn't why you're blue.
No, but that isn't the point.

Then what is the point?
I am at my threshold.
It takes only the smallest stress
before part of me collapses.

But when you calve,
you get smaller. Some day,
you will not be here.
No, I will not.

So, you are dying then.

No. I am giving myself away.
Or, I am fulfilling my wish
to cut the dead from myself,
to relieve myself of the burden
of attachment. Some ice begs
to split from me.

Is that not the fault
of the sun? Or of us?

Maybe. But the sun won't stop.
And you won't stop.
I un-family the same as you:
We cleave together. Then,
we cleave apart.

Neck-Steering

I grew up with his hand locking my head in place. At night,
I feel my shoulders hunch around my pillow.
Chiropractic videos make me shiver and cringe.
The way he'd grab my neck and shake it
was his form of embrace. His hug was a shackle.
When he was angry, he'd steer me by my neck, my whole body
swiveling to catch up to my head. Once, he did it to save me
from slipping out of a rollercoaster
I was too small to ride. More than once,
it was to throw me somewhere
before his hands could form a weapon.

A Feast of Ortolans

For years, my father hid
   in the attic of our home.
As if he had draped over himself
   the tent of a napkin,
as if to shield himself
   from the gaze of the almighty god,
he stayed under the gabled roof.
   Every day, he continued the ritual:
he drowned the songbird,
   placed it whole into his mouth,
bit down hard on the neck.

After Reading Lundy Bancroft, Domestic Abuse Counselor

I've been under the thumb of my father forever.
I know the colors of his anger. Now,
I seek out harm from men.

He was made to rehearse the violence,
to reenact the worship of fist to flesh,
the self-same choreography repeating:

My grandfather strikes my father for inadequacy.
My father strikes me for shame.
I, without child, strike myself.

We do this over and over
until each of us is satisfied
with his punishment.

Last Phone Call with Grandpa Ruben

It was a week before his birthday in August,
a date I still haven't memorized. Last year,
he stopped sending birthday gifts because I never called.
I get it. He's lonely. The cancer has gotten worse. The clichés
about mortality are setting in, and he's facing a kingdom of regret.
But I know his game. I know how his love takes the form
of transactions. Attention costs money to him. He's dangled support
over my parents for years. He's done the same to me. I'm still unclear
on what love is, but I'm certain it isn't that. He calls me
and tells me he's disappointed in me for changing my name.
He's consulted "the family," strangers I've never met, never heard from,
never knew existed, and they're all ashamed of me.
It's a lack of respect: throwing away tradition, throwing away heritage.
What history do I belong to? I don't know where my skin comes from.
But I know the color it bruises.

Chekhov's Guns

In my father's two safes are twenty-three guns
and ten barrels. Reloaded ammunition.
Fresh shells. Sights. Padded cases.
He must have sold some since Florida.
But by now you know this. I wrote it,
and it appeared. Just like I wrote my wish,
and it came true. Pay attention to the details:
the sister, the guns, the grandfather, the father,
the fists, the knives, the blood, the sex, the anger.

The court inquires about the firearms, illegal
in the possession of a felon, but
they're in Mom's name, so she sells them.
The money goes in a separate account for now.
My father posts bail. No, wait,
my grandfather posts bail for him. A whole
thirty thousand dollars in cash. A hotel. A cab to the house
with a police escort. He takes his truck, the belongings
Mom packed in suitcases. The cop a wall between them,
so she never sees his face. But she hears him yell.
Details: on the floor of the room where his luggage lay
is the sweater Mom knit for him.

For days we worry he's still in town, then I worry
he's left town. His other option is his father, only
forty-five minutes from me. I have to remind myself
he doesn't have my door code. He doesn't have a key.
For days and days we check credit statements

for any clue. More details: the debit card,
the phone bill, the bank account, the gas tank of the truck,
the distance between Minnesota and Nebraska.

I call my professors. I might have to disappear.
I plan on driving up to Mom. I wonder if I'd pass him on I-80.
After my father calls me, he calls my sister.
He speaks to her for forty-two minutes according to T-Mobile.
I have no idea what happens between them,
but Mom warns Sarah not to talk about each parent with the other.
I almost want to tell her she's stupid for giving him time.
I should know better. Details: Daddy's girl.

I know Sarah tells Mom she's not surprised. He's hit her too.
Then a purchase at a Walmart in Omaha. Details, details.
Now I know he's with my grandfather and all my grandfather's
guns, too.

DANCO

(Domestic Abuse No Contact Order)

Of all things, a toothbrush. Then jeans.
Though first it was the glucometer,
and to prevent guilt, Mom mailed it.
But then it was more. Some kind of weak apology,
then begging, then blaming, a two-second video
of my father's face that was probably supposed to be
a photo. A countable number of offenses forwarded
to the police department. Every text laced
with rage, every notification a threat. His name,
its own kind of torment.

Auto-da-Fé

When the pyre is lit,
the criminal shouts to the crowd
gathered below. He proclaims
his innocence. The smoke rises.

The skin, which feels the holiest of pains,
turns to ash. Then: numbness.
But his breath burns. Smoke
and ember eat away the tenderness
of the throat and lungs.

He is a spectacle, quickening his death
through his screams. He believes himself
a martyr. What cruel things everyone has said
about him. How foolish they'll feel
when he comes down in his golden chariot.

O why, then, does the crackle of firewood
surge so loudly in his ears?

Self-Portrait Without Father

Sitting outside of the banh mi shop, Mom
calls to tell me she served him divorce papers.
He tried to serve her first, but he didn't fill them out right.

Forgot to sign it. Didn't get an attorney. He proves
he's a letdown. I've already lived so many years
independent of him. This is nothing new.

In Minnesota, Mom has already taken down the pictures.
We had a whole wall of family photos. Now he hallway
is full of nails and gaps where frames were hung.

I've been made Mom's beneficiary. Little by little,
erasing him. I've made plans to erase his last name, too.

Then I do. I swear in front of a court, and my name
is transmogrified. A woman in Nebraska hits her gavel,
and it is made so.

I was told by my grandfather, after twenty-seven years of living,
that our name came from colonizers, from conquistadors
who settled in Sonora, Mexico. Our name was Basque,

a language, as marvelous as it is, still born in Europe.
I'm eating a banh mi, its own relic of colonization:
French bread, pâté.

I am thinking about the name erased in Sonora.
What name did they have before it became ██████?
What name could I have been?

I practice my new signature on a napkin. I practice
on printer paper. I try different styles of print and cursive.
I bring the paper with all my tries to Mom
and ask her which one she likes best.

A World Where You Labor Twice as Much

In Mexico, I am writing an essay that will receive praise from my professor
and then a note that tells me to write something else for the assignment.
But I don't know that yet. All I know is that I'm writing twenty pages
weaving grief and disability and poetry together. And it's fine. I'm working,
and I love the work I'm doing, though it will end up in a drawer later. But
then I go into the kitchen in this vacation rental Mom got with a friend
for all of us to go down and work on our projects, like a self-made writing retreat.
I go into the kitchen because a local chef is coming for dinner. We eat. The chef
is kind and funny. He makes a ceviche with a black *recado* from the Yucatán,
and we're all impressed. I was happily sated. But K turns to me and asks me,

"Why are you so *angry*? Why stay so *angry* all the time?"

I know that K knows my father tried to kill Mom. I know
she knows he tried to crush her throat. I know she knows how close I am
to Mom. So, what was the question again? Mom is at the table with us
and looks like she wants to know too. I count on six fingers each coffin nail
I have somehow survived. I call them my tragic backstories. Why am I so *angry*?
Anne Carson asked, "Where can I put it down?" Well,
I'm asking where I can burn it down. I want to burn it into something
like I got burnt for thirty years of my life. Why should I be the better person?

I've never lied about who I am. I've told you I hate a lot of things.
I've been cruel in my own ways too. I haven't always apologized.
But why stay *angry*? I can tell you, at the very least, it's so I don't forget. And forget
about forgiving. That's never been my style, no. I chisel my grudges into stone.
If you forget, I'll do the remembering for the both of us.

The First Christmas I Don't Have to Dream My Father Dead or Gone

with a first line adapted from Frank Bidart

is exorcism.

I leave my shoes in the living room. I pour wine
without a comment. I take out cookbooks

and plan the next month in stews and curries,
breads, cookies, meats, cheeses. I

don't turn down the TV or turn up the heat.
I grade my students' papers without Jack

in my tea. I keep my headphones on all day,
and no one stares at me until I take them off.

I write notes to myself: Write a poem. Think
about the babka recipe. Sharpen knives. Get

the ornaments and such out of the garage.
Oh, and I can park in the garage, so I do.

I do as I please, though each freedom
is clarified by the ghost-vise of his hand.

Pecha Kucha: After Packing My Father's Room

after Terrance Hayes

[watches]

I think it was about two thousand dollars' worth after I tallied them up.
Some brand called Invicta. Ugly things. Huge and bulky.
Star Wars, Army, whatever. A Casio, a knockoff Fitbit.
Paid for by money to get him out of the house, to find a hobby.

[clothes]

Camo everywhere. Nothing that fit him.
Hunting gear. Clothes he might have worn once.
When was the last time he wore that bolo tie?
I can't remember seeing him in a dress shirt.

[hangers]

Wide enough they don't fit in a box. Wooden.
Plastic ones bound with tape so they could get packed.
Auntie Vicki wondering how he had so many.
Mom telling her this was only one closet.

[colored pencils]

Practically untouched. He always thought he was artistic
because he copied a few things out of the newspaper.
A man whose face was a fingerprint—
he got it tattooed on his arm and thought I'd like it.

[moose rack]

Sure, he did kill this one. Fed us for a year in Alaska.
Every home needed a wall for the trophy.
But this home didn't have a high enough stud to drill into.
It's been on the floor since, holding a bow I've never seen strung.

[magazines]

As much as he resented his hoarder mother, he can't let go.
Year-old issues about reloading ammunition. Building guns.
Buying parts. Customizing scopes. Did he ever reread them?
They gathered dust in the corner.

[pipe]

I packed his pipe mere hours after learning how much he
smoked.
I never smelled it on him. Never caught him in the act.
But I held it up and laughed until Mom said, *You wonder why*
he spent his time in the garage while one kid molested the other?

[shoes]

Pristine. Leather. Still smelled new. Didn't look like
the soles were broken in. Hunting boots.
Loafers. Tennis shoes. Boat shoes. Dress shoes.
I've always been thankful I was a half-size too small.

[model cars]

Four whole display cases of die-cast cars,
1:18 size, but don't quote me. Some he painted
and assembled himself. I wanted to help when I was little,
but he chased me out of the garage.

[telescope]

I don't know why Mom is so concerned about its care.
We don't need to spend the money on special packing.
It's not our problem anymore. After the divorce,
it'll be his to deal with. He never used it anyway.

[gun case]

Empty. But there's a pellet gun. It's the only gun
that survived the purge. The only legal one a felon can have.
I'm not sure why Mom decided not to pawn it with the rest.
Why hand a violent man a machine of violence?

[recliner]

Honestly, it's a comfortable chair. The dogs like it too.
But it takes up too much space. Doesn't fit anywhere well.
Wrong color. Won't match the room after redecorating.
Something about it still carries his impression.

[TV]

He demanded it in the counterpetition. Everything
in his so-called man cave. With a no-contact order in place,
did he really think he would get to come in and rummage
as he pleased? He'd be happy with NASCAR and Fox News alone.

[bible]

Perhaps the most ironic thing here. Books about saints.
A guide to Catholic devotions. Called Mom a hypocrite
when Texas made miscarriages "murder" and she said it wasn't right.
For him, god was another gun to aim.

[another gun]

I've lost count now, but I think this is the fourth AR-15.
Do you know how easy it is to order parts and build one?
They're called ghost guns. No serial number. No background check.
Felons like him have free reign. Add to Cart, then Purchase.

[weed]

Mom found his stash after I left. Bottom drawer
in his side table. Got all over her fingers,
and she was pissed. I don't even want to add up
all the money she spent appeasing him.

[boxes with my handwriting]

I hope he recognizes it. My mostly print / slightly cursive.
Hope he sees I didn't write "tackle boxes," wrote
"fishing junk" instead. I kept the snark to a minimum,
but I was so angry the whole time.

[boxes with my aunt's handwriting]

Vicki wrote "ED" on every box. Not just pants,
ED pants. His possessions we were tasked with cleaning up.
ED this, ED that. If you want it your way, then have it.
He probably won't recognize her writing. He can wonder about it.

[boxes with Mom's handwriting]

Mom packed his family's china carefully. Marked it with his
mother's
family name. She liked the cut crystal, but I hated the plates.
There's enough dead peoples' things in this house
without adding his dead people too.

[hardwood floors]

Underneath that ugly gray carpet. The wood has some paint,
a lot of dirt. Carpet nails. Mom sent a picture with my aunt victorious,
arms pumped up, foot on ripped-up folds of carpet. It'll be lovely
after some sanding, after some wax, after some good ol' TLC.

It's the Little Things

for Mom

like curried tuna fish the day after
getting rid of the grandfather clock
rearranging the living room
trashing the joke mugs
returning the Christmas gift parka
regifting the sweater you knit
having your son cook goat and lamb and chickpeas and
  ginger and curry and goat cheese and
not putting the girl scout cookies in the freezer
tossing the blue cheese dressing out
not overfeeding the dogs
taking down his photos
making the extra room an office
planting flowers in the backyard
parking in the garage
watching romcoms and detective shows
turning the upstairs into a studio
having dinner parties and friends over
painting the front door yellow
all the little things you don't notice
one by one piling up until you look around
and notice how much more light there is in the room

Don't Worry, I'm Still Mad, and I Know Who the Villain Is

My cat supervises me from her water bowl
as I scoop her shit. I'm upstairs with a glass of wine
and an empty screen. I spent last night
in Minneapolis seeing friends.
Today, I drove back home two hours
listening to a podcast about gossip—
the kind of gossip that happens to a friend
of a friend, but not you. Not in your world.
In my world, though, I can see the rumors take flight.
Spider-silk tendrils of he-said-she-said,
little networking ants tunneling through the drama.
And at the center isn't quite me. Not me.
Mom. Edmund. I'm somewhere close though.
A bunch of little things: colors of blankets,
scented candles, food. Innocuous vapors
of discontent made suddenly real: He
wouldn't let me. He always commented on it.
He never. He couldn't. He hated. He wasn't.
Not as if I disagree. In fact, I add to the list.
Give me a verb, and I'll find his favorite negative.
It does get old, but I can't stop. Neither of us can stop.

Some spiders parachute: they let loose a sticky silk anchor
on the wind and let it take them elsewhere. Wish
it were me. Wish it weren't my gossip.
But here we are, bitching about an open door in winter

"letting the heat out" while we unload groceries
or corral the dogs in the months of her lowest bills.
The little angers do add up. Or multiply.
Whatever math make things exponential,
that's what it is. The angers exponent,
until you're in the kitchen, two maws agape,
echoing damnations back and forth
across snickerdoodles and pies.

Speculations About Anger

after Toi Derricotte

I

All things die in me.
I spoke with anger to kill things.
I speak with anger to do the killing.
Anger is my tool, a handle
I've worn to a familiar grip.

II

I have denied it. I have masked
it. I have sung or danced around
it. I have placed it where I promised
I wouldn't. I have never let it breathe
as I have breathed. Never let it
dash itself on a rock, lest I.

III

It is a measure by which I measure.
I mean, it is circular. Recursive.
Recursive, meaning
it runs into itself again. Runs back
to the source, to the hand which stretches the tape
and marks the farthest extension.

IV

It stains me. It changed my skin.
It changed my clothes. I walk,
and it shadows. I can't be rid of it.
I refuse to rid it.

V

It eludes me. No,
not the feeling of it.
The ending of it.

VI

I have spent so long
peering into shadows
to find the body
that casts the shadow
in order to exorcise it.

I have reached into dark boxes
full of unnamable objects,
felt every contour until
I could give them names,
could trace their histories,
could pull them out and set them aside.

VII

I am an angry person.
I am my anger.

VIII

I asked Why or How
but I never got an answer.
Now, I ask Where.
Where do I put it? Where
do I use it? Or Who.
Who needs it. Who gets it.

IX

It is my earliest memory.
My twin, cradle companion.
Now, I sit at the edge of my bed,
watch the glass kettle boil, watch
placid waters rumble up.
Every day I boil water. Some days
the heat is on, but the water runs out.

X

I am angry but not violent,
at least I don't think so.
But I've been called cruel,
and I've admitted to it.
Some nights I dream
of shattering things—
precious or mundane—
any breakable thing.
Whatever I hold in the dream,
I dream it destroyed.
I wake and fear myself.
I fear my anger.

XI

I've sat in a mirrored room
and spoken about anger.
Anger was in the room with us,
and only I could see the ghost.
I tell you, it doesn't leave me.
The other person compliments me,
my understanding of anger.
No, you see, all I did
was move it from my claws
to my eyes.

XII

Maybe it is a ghost.
Not the shadow I thought. Maybe
it has unfinished business. Maybe
it won't go 'til I get even. I tell you,
I tell you,
I'm afraid of my anger. I'm afraid
I'll be alone without it.

XIII

Make me a promise, Anger.
Doesn't matter what,
only bind me to you forever.

Credits and Notes

A special thanks to the editors of the following publications who have given a home to poems in this manuscript (sometimes in different forms or with different titles, and under a previous name):

The Acentos Review: "Sheep's Brain," "Worship," and "Touch-Starved"
Assaracus: A Journal of Gay Poetry: "Fear"
Barrelhouse Magazine: "Knife Spell"
The Cincinnati Review: "High Quality Tattoo 8 × 6″ Blank Practice Skin for Beginners and Experienced Artists"
Drunk Monkeys: "Sarah as Grendel" and "Jeff Forces Me to Have Sex with Strangers, Then Calls Me a Cheating Slut"
Five:2:One Magazine: "Boy Found Dead"
The Florida Review: "Trajectory" and "Pecha Kucha: After Packing My Father's Room"
Glass: A Journal of Poetry: "Lengua" and "Jackhammer"
Gulf Coast: "Kindness"
Moon City Review: "Her Bedroom"
River Styx: "Doll Play"
The Shade Journal: "Daddy Porn" (Many thanks to Luther Hughes for guidance.)
Waxwing: "On My Birthday I Witness a Car Accident"

The word *oarlock* in "Sarah as Grendel" is a gift from Jackie Genovese.

Italicized lines of "Boy Found Dead" come from various March 2018 news headlines in which the phrase "boy found dead" is found.

"Sarah as Grendel" is after Hannah Cohen.

Acknowledgments

First and foremost, I want to thank my mom, Dr. Kimmie Shannon, the most important person in my life, for being my rock and my foundation. I would not have been able to write these poems without your unwavering support, even when the poems hurt you. You have always been my inspiration and my North Star. I love you.

To all my teachers and mentors, past and present: Cathy Windish, Rachel Jamison Webster, Laura Passin, Kwame Dawes, Marvin Bell, Ellen Bass, Dorianne Laux, Joe Millar, Eduardo C. Corral, Debra Gwartney, Vievee Francis, Stacey Waite, Timothy Schaffert, Rebecca Buller, and Hope Wabuke. Thank you for believing in me, my words, my memories. Thank you for your guidance. Thank you for your critiques, even when I didn't want to hear them. Thank you for cheering me on endlessly. Each of you has left an indelible mark on this collection.

To my friends and/or fellow poets: So many of you have touched this book at one time or another and left it better. I cannot thank you enough, but I will try.

To Sarah Lowe, Hannah Kraus, Ryan Knutson, Rob Parise: I love you. I would be nothing without you in my life.

To Michele Bombardier, Jennifer Saunders, Nancy Miller Gomez: My poetry Moms! I love you with my whole heart. Thank you for making me cry in the cafeteria.

To Ava Nathaniel Winter, Jamaica Baldwin, Katie Marya, Jessica Poli, Celie Knudsen, Charlotte Kupsh, Erika Luckert, Jason McCormick: Thank you for making Nebraska a place to thrive in. Thank you for your love and community.

To my *Cotton Xenomorph* family: E. K. Anderson, Chloe N. Clark, Hannah Cohen, Erin Schmiel, Chris Corlew, Kanika Lawton: Thank you for supporting me at every point in this journey.

To Luna Rey Hall, Mary Thorson, Otis Houston, Florian Dotti, Jeeae Chang, Charity Dewing: May we one day empty the hotel bar of champagne again.

To Jericho Brown, Robert James Russell, Todd Dillard: Thank you for your friendship, encouragement, support.

To the Last Minute Poets and our December 30/30 group: Thank you for reading 90 percent of the first drafts of the poems in this book. You were instrumental in the writing of this manuscript. Your positivity is rare and beautiful.

To the crews at Stumptgamers and the Judgies: Thank you for keeping me company through multiple degrees and years of revision. Thank you for cheering me on endlessly.

Another tremendous thank you to Laura Passin: You mean the world to me. You changed me the moment I met you. You showed me what poetry could be. I guide my ship by your light, praise Theia.

To all my other friends and supporters: I hold you in my heart. My most heartfelt thanks to you as well.